Sell Like A Savage

Contents

Introduction	3
Selling with your Ears	6
The Art of Self-Deprecation	12
Yes! Messaging does Matter	17
Personality Trait Selling? BS	23
When to Step Back	29
The Value of No	35
Passion	42
Burying the Competition	47
Coffee is for CLOSERS	53

Introduction

I am not a writer, professor, or nationally known businessman. I am different, and that is perfectly okay because I know I can provide a fresh perspective for the typical sales professional. I am just a normal, everyday guy (although my wife may not agree with normal).

I have read multiple sales, management, and leadership books, and I have learned a ton from them. But I always felt a little bit of disconnect. These books, while effective, often drug the story on for too long, making it hard to stay focused on the message they were trying to deliver. I didn't have a personal connection to the writer, and at times it felt more like theory rather than real-world applications or results.

A former coach of mine once told me, "In order to be successful you need two things; you need to be lucky, and you need to be good." Looking back at my career so far, I would say it has been successful, although at times it has looked a little shaky! I have been extremely lucky in my career. I have been in the right place, at the right time. I have had good mentors. I have had people take a risk on me. While all of these things have contributed to my success, I have also leveraged my luck to snowball my success. I have had many late nights and long drives, some leading to big deals, and others ending with a door in my face. But with a little bit of luck and a lot of hard work, I was fortunate to win Rookie of the Year in 2014 and Rep of the Year in 2016 for an organization that is worth around a billion dollars. This company took a huge chance on me (I wasn't even shaving when they hired me!), and I was not about to let them down.

In this book, I discuss nine unique tools to help you understand how to grow your sales. Some of you probably perform very well in various areas highlighted in this book, and several of you may do things a little differently than me. That is one of many reasons why I love the sales industry; there are so many ways to get from point A to point B. This book identifies the key skills that I believe will set you apart from the crowd.

I understand the typical sales professional is busy. This book is designed to be short, informative, and concise, while providing you with effective strategies to improve your sales - just like your typical sales call! You should be able to crush this read in under an hour. I am pumped you have made it this far in my book, so I am going to shut up and let you read. I hope this gives you the opportunity to learn one or two things to help you grow your business.

Selling with your Ears

"Just shut up and listen!"

These were some of the first words I heard as I entered sales training class as a 22 year-old, fresh out of college, at a prominent medical device company. The man proclaiming these words looked like my grandfather who had maybe enjoyed one-too-many glasses of scotch over the years. While stress had clearly taken its toll on him over his career, I found myself listening intently to his every word. And boy was I glad I was naïve enough to pay attention. I would later learn that the worn-out looking man was one of the most successful sales reps in the history of our company.

His words of advice weren't spoken to anyone in our class directly. He happened to be telling a story to a colleague, and he was frustrated that most salespeople just "talk" and never listen. Before you assume I'd been eavesdropping, let me be clear; the man was so animated that his voice vibrated off the marble floors as if he were using a bullhorn. But I had been so intrigued by what I'd heard, that later in the afternoon I approached him and picked his brain. I specifically asked him about the story I, and the rest of the world, had overheard. He looked at me and said, "Successful sales people don't sell by talking; they sell by listening. **_They sell with their ears._**"

That statement could not be truer on so many levels. In the last seven years of selling, I have learned this lesson many times over. When we get hired, we are pumped full of information about all the amazing things our companies can offer. And being the excited, and often extroverted, people that we are, we jump to share this information with as many potential and existing customers as we can. Our enthusiasm for our products or services is essential to be successful in sales, but too often this enthusiasm causes us to make a huge mistake. We all do it. We talk too much.

Talking too much in a sales conversation is often counterproductive and actually prevents us from being able to effectively sell. There are a few major reasons this strategy does not help.

First, we often have limited time with our customer. This means we need to take advantage of the little time we do have and obtain as much information as possible from the customer. We should still dominate and direct the conversation, but we should do this by asking specific questions targeting the pain points to further the sales process.

Second, in order to be successful we need to understand our customers' needs. We do this by asking questions. Picture yourself peeling away at an onion; when you identify a customer's problem, ask more questions to help identify the next layer until you get to the center of that problem. Do not be the person that pukes out features and benefits of your product without listening to a word your customer has to say.

Third, it is disingenuous and unauthentic to talk more than our customers. You should aim to make them feel important. Be excited and engaged in the conversation. We never want to be the first people talking about our kids or our golf game.

Selling with our ears is a needs analysis approach, which can be extremely effective. A needs analysis approach uncovers specific customer needs one question at a time. By listening closely to our customers' answers, we can identify pain points and circle back to these points when the time is right to go through our brief elevator pitch. This strategy certainly isn't designed to close a deal, but it is intended to advance the sale to the next stage or create action items around a future visit.

One of my favorite parts of unpeeling the onion is uncovering how much potential business actually exists. I had scheduled a meeting with one of my prospective surgeons to sell a product meant to treat a specific condition; I did not get any of his business at the time. My manager decided to fly up and join the meeting due to the perceived opportunity. At the end of the meeting I asked him how many patients he treated with this condition. He answered truthfully, "Not many". I was bummed out. Ready to pack it in for the day, I stood up and shook his hand, thanked him for his time and set up a time to demo our product. As we walked out, my manager asked, "How many patients is "not many" for you in a week?" The doctor replied back, "Probably two to four a week." A light bulb went off in my head; my definition of not many could definitely be different than my customer's. This could actually be a homerun! I ended up getting his business, and he was one of my busiest surgeons. The point of sharing this experience is, I almost disregarded a huge opportunity because I didn't finish unpeeling the onion. I made assumptions and stopped asking questions. ***Always continue to unpeel!***

"What if I am asked to do a presentation in front of many individuals? How is it possible to ask questions in a presentation?" I have heard this question multiple times from peers and trainees, and my simple answer is a quote from my high school basketball coach – "Excuses are for losers." There are plenty of opportunities to ask questions in a presentation to uncover pain points. The excuses stop here.

Before a presentation, find out as much as you possibly can about the company you are presenting to. Find out why they scheduled you to present. They must think you have a solution to one of their problems if they have allowed you to take some of their time. Determine their expectations and tailor your presentation around what you find out. After you have done this, you can start to identify areas to ask needs-based questions. If you can turn this into organic conversation, that is fantastic – you have done well!

We ultimately sell by listening to our customer. We listen to their needs, their problems, and their successes. We ask targeted questions to obtain specific information to accomplish our goals of the conversation. By listening, we can better understand our customer and how we need to sell to them in order to help them solve their problem.

Be calm, be engaged, go slow, and ask many questions. Be analytical and precise, like an animal stalking its prey. ***Listen like a savage!***

Key Action Items For "Selling with your Ears"

1. Research your customer to understand their business
2. Ask targeted questions
3. Keep asking questions based on the answers you receive
4. Find pain points by listening
5. Leverage the pain points in an elevator pitch to advance the sale

The Art of Self-Deprecation

"Huh, weird title of this chapter, not sure what it means or how it can help me sell…"

That might be the first reaction most people have to this chapter's title. However, self-deprecation can be a useful trait in sales. I will discuss self-deprecation and how it branches out to touch many aspects of a sale, specifically in developing relationships and earning our customers' trust.

I had no idea what self-deprecation was until I was in my sophomore year of college. I had a teammate – I will call him "Josh" – that was the Picasso of self-deprecation. Inwardly, Josh knew he was the best golfer in every tournament he entered; however, he would never come off as cocky or arrogant. Rather, he would joke around, dog his golf game, and make fun of himself to keep the mood light. I would listen to him tell other teams he couldn't make a putt outside of two feet and shouldn't be allowed to travel to the next tournament. But he would always go out and perform at a high level, and would dominate most tournaments. Not surprisingly, Josh is experiencing an extremely successful sales career, and was recently promoted to Regional Sales Manager in a fast-growing, service-orientated company that has close to 1,000 employees.

When selling, it is important to remember that people rarely buy from vendors they do not like. This is especially true if the sales cycle is long because we are constantly communicating with our customer in order to meet their needs. We need to **_be likeable, relatable, and humble_** in the sales cycle; this adds value to our customer because it makes us tolerable to work with over a long period of time.

Self-deprecation truly is an art. We are walking a fine line between being professional and being relatable. If we are too self-deprecating, we can come across as unprofessional, which can lead to poor credibility and our customer not trusting us to do the job. We have to be self-aware, because it is essential to know the right time to leverage this trait.

I typically find self-deprecation to be most effective when I am first meeting a customer, when I am finding out what hobbies they enjoy, and when I am closing – yes, I use this as a closing mechanism at times!

One of my go-to self-deprecating lines (which is a true statement, I swear) comes up when customers ask how my wife is doing. I usually respond, "She hasn't divorced me yet, so we are all good!" Other times, customers find out I played college golf, and they ask questions about where I have played, what my best score is or if I have had a hole-in-one. I definitely have not had a hole-in-one; you have to be good at golf to do that. And when asked about my best score, I usually refer to my mini golf score. But there are times when self-deprecation is not the best tactic. For instance, I tend to direct the conversation away from where I have played golf. I most certainly would not tell most people I have played some of the best golf courses in the country; I mean how relatable is that? However, if I were one-on-one with a customer that tells me they played Pebble Beach last weekend, I would leverage my experiences as a relationship-building tool, no doubt!

It is all about understanding our customer and our situation and being self-aware. This goes hand-in-hand with the first chapter; if we are asking questions first, it allows us to judge the situation and be as effective as possible when building relationships. Being relatable and having humility are key components to building relationships and continuing to sell to our customers. Maintaining confidence without being arrogant puts us in a better position to sell more effectively. Self-deprecation can conquer all of these tasks when used correctly.

If you haven't used this tactic in the past, I would definitely practice this before using it in the marketplace. An easy way to implement this is with friends; they are typically interested in how our life is going or what is new. Practice your pitch and make it your own. Have the self-awareness to **_self-deprecate like a savage!_**

Key Action Items for "The Art of Self-Deprecation"

1. Practice this to make it your own, but make it intentional
2. Identify customers/prospects this would be most effective with
3. Find a theme and stick to it

4. Implement this in the marketplace with a solidified relationship
5. Execute this with a prospect or lead to gain their trust

Yes! Messaging Does Matter

"Messaging is so fluffy, it is a wasteful sales tactic that provides no value."

That is exactly what went through my head when I was an ignorant, young sales rep entering the business world. As a matter of fact, I don't think I used this tool for the first two years of my selling career. Luckily, I received a bad review from my manager and that CHANGED!

I was driving through the rural Midwest with my new manager, who had been riding along with me for a couple of days. I was coming up on my one-year anniversary and had hit my goal in all but one month. I thought I was doing well and wasn't too worried about him coming to town. I guess I should have been more concerned. He gave me an Account Visit Evaluation based on the visits he observed, during which he broke down my sales skills. He pointed out that the entire time he'd been with me, I never managed to have a single pre-meditated message in any of the accounts we visited – not one! He looked me in the eye and told me I was better off staying home if I was not going to have a message and be intentional in my accounts. Instead of getting upset about this feedback, I listened as he coached me on how to deliver an effective message and we devised a plan for future account visits. To this day, that was the best review I have received. Sure, I had been doing things well, but there were many areas I needed to improve in to make my success sustainable. Messaging was one of these areas.

When I was visiting my accounts I always felt like there wasn't enough to talk about; we didn't have any new products, insurance networks, marketing information, etc. I also used the excuse that I saw my accounts every other week – they already knew everything about us. Again, I was WRONG! Messaging is an extremely effective tool, especially when we have repeat customers that we build long-term relationships with.

Let's break down how to become a savage in the message game. To start, you need to get a pen and a piece of paper ***and write down 10-15***

items that your company does really well, better than most of your competitors. The messaging list can include company stories, company history, marketing information, product information, etc. – whatever you think highlights the benefits of your company. There isn't a right or wrong answer in this exercise; the most important step to create the message is to make the list.

Once you identify a messaging list, devise a plan for how you will communicate the message to your customer. If you see your customer quite often, you will most likely deliver your message in person, whereas if you see your customer a couple times per year, you may need to reach out via phone or email. Keep in mind, like most sales-related activities, anything that can be performed in person will prove to be more effective.

After you have completed your messaging list and determined how you are going to share the message, you need to find a way to bring the message with you. A former colleague once suggested that our district put our message on brightly colored paper and have it laminated. These are both fantastic ideas. A bright color sticks out from the possible mess of product information floating around in our cars. I found the lamination beneficial for two reasons. The first, and arguably most important reason, was to make sure when I spilled something on the paper it didn't get ruined! The second reason was I could take a dry erase marker and cross off the messages that I had recently completed with certain customers. It was an effective technique that worked very well for me and for others in my district. If you don't like the idea of carrying around more papers, it is also conducive to put the messaging list in email format and send it to yourself or have it in a notepad.

Messaging is really about initiating organic conversation that leads into other aspects of our business that we can sell. To give you an example, one of my messages was how well established our insurance networks were. I would share with providers that about 95% of the patients in my territory were covered by insurances that my company was in network with. This always sparked a light bulb for providers about difficult insurance networks they were dealing with, or other recent dealings with insurance. The conversation always ended in a place I didn't necessarily intend it to go (all good, no worries!), and I walked out of many repeat customer offices with new information and pain points.

I like to use a technique when beginning my message. It goes something like this. "Have I told you about how we were founded? If I have, just tell me to shut my mouth and we can move on!" This starts the conversation without an aggressive sales pitch and comes across very relatable while adding value and information for the customer. I challenge you to find an effective opening line that will travel with you to multiple customers.

Messaging works, trust me – let's provide value for our customers when we speak to them. Don't be the rep that goes on the milk run just to fill out our weekly activity report to satisfy management. ***Be intentional; message like a savage!***

Key Action Items for "Yes! Messaging Does Matter"

1. Evaluate what your company does really well
2. Narrow the list to 10 – 15 items you want to message on
3. Get organized – build the list, develop an electronic copy
4. Devise your messaging strategy via in-person visits or email

5. Execute the messaging plan with solid relationships, then branch out

Personality Trait Selling? BS

"What does your Myers-Briggs Personality Test say about how you should sell to Dr. Jones?"

This was a question I found myself faced with in the middle of an account visit. I was on my way into a large office with over a dozen physicians. As a progressive clinic that provided exceptional medical care for their patients, they often had a variety of sales reps around. A pharmaceutical rep caught me in the hallway, and she asked me that question. I was a deer in the headlights. There is a personality test to figure out how to sell?

Yes, I am so naïve at times that I had no idea that personality trait selling was a real thing. This is how it works. You take an individualized personality test, which can be subjective depending on your own self-awareness. Once you submit this, you can evaluate different components of your personality; different tests may focus on different traits. The other piece to the puzzle is you must also input information about each of your decision makers from your various accounts; this can be a huge gamble if you don't know them as well as you should. The final results will come with suggestions on how to sell to each of your decision makers. Essentially, you get a personalized sales approach for each individual.

I may be in the minority with my opinion on this technique, and that is fine, but I am going to lay out the reasons I think this is BS.

If you need a personality trait test to tell you how to sell to your customer, I hate to tell you that I think you may be in the wrong career! This goes back to the previous chapters of this book, specifically "Selling with your Ears". If you are listening to your customers, you will learn about their personal lives, how they react to certain situations and the problems they are currently having with their business. By listening to them, you will be able to understand how to sell to them.

I had two fantastic surgeons in the "middle of nowhere" Kansas. They were about 70 miles apart and both were the only specialty surgeons of their kind in their respective towns. While their careers sound very similar, they were both extremely different surgeons; their personalities were worlds apart, they had different hobbies and they took different career paths to get where they were. Oh, and one of the doctors was a HUGE Republican, while the other doctor was a MASSIVE Democrat.

It happened to be 2012 when I discovered this information about them. This was when President Obama was facing Mitt Romney in the Presidential elections. I would typically drive out to see these doctors on the same day. I would show up for a meeting with doctor #1 and, not 25 seconds in, would hear, "Can you believe this Obama guy? If we re-elect him the world will light on fire." I would then hop in my car, make the 70-mile drive to my next appointment and immediately hear, "Romney can't lead this country; he's makes too much money!"

I have a couple rules that I know are fairly common in the sales community. I do not speak about religion or politics because decision makers can, and often will, base decisions specifically on personal opinions, such as politics. However, after talking with these guys for a few months, I learned they wanted to vent more than anything. Patients would come in during their clinic and complain about the current landscape in politics, and the surgeons, using that same rule of "don't talk religion or politics" with their patients, needed to air their grievances to a "neutral" party. I embraced my role as their sounding board, and I ended up learning more about politics than watching television or listening to the radio ever taught me! And, most importantly, I kept my personal opinions to myself and would nod my head along with what they said.

The point of this story is not to lecture you on politics. It is to emphasize the importance of not making the moment about yourself; **_be a chameleon, understand your customer_** and learn more about who they are. Leverage that understanding to build a relationship, and then ultimately leverage the relationship to obtain business or generate more business. Does a personality test tell us what was discussed above? I can't say for sure, but I certainly don't think so.

My dad took me to a Triple A baseball game when I was 10 years old. In between the first and second inning they started shooting hot dogs out of a cannon. My dad leaned over and said, "I'm not a fan of gimmicks, but they need butts in seats." That was the first time I'd heard the word "gimmick". Do you see where I am going here? Is personality trait selling a gimmick? I believe so. It is intended to give the appearance that something is easier than it really is, but ultimately this is an inconsistent short cut.

Understanding our customers is not an easy thing to do, and understanding how to sell to them is not easy either. There are customers that need to be pushed to get information, while others like to joke around and some are more serious and engaged. We need to have the ability to decipher our customer's personality ourselves through conversation and use the information we learn to determine the best way to sell to them.

This chapter is all about how to build relationships and sell to decision makers with different personalities. When I approach a new customer, I usually start the conversation with a few questions to get us going and often utilize some self-deprecation to lighten the mood. If I don't get a great response, I know I have a more serious and direct customer on my hands and change my approach. The important thing is to remain aware of your customer's reactions and to be adaptable in your conversation.

Don't take the easy way out; put in the time, effort and hard work to get to know your customers. Understanding our customers' personalities takes time and patience. It is a long process to build a relationship with our customer, and then ultimately understand how to sell to that specific individual. ***Build relationships like a savage!***

Key Action Items for "Personality Trait Selling? BS"

1. Leverage the hard work and relationship developed to sell to each customer's individual personality
2. Determine the most effective sales mechanisms
3. Devise a plan and write down goals or milestones you want to achieve
4. Execute the plan with your customer but be flexible if it deviates
5. Have fun – close the sale(s) with the chosen plan

When to Step Back

"You don't have to be the smartest person in the room to be the best salesperson."

It is hard for salespeople to acknowledge that they need the support of others in the company. We don't want to show any signs of "weakness" within our company or to our customers. However, I would argue that asking for the input of your other team members actually demonstrates your self-awareness and integrity. It shows the customer that you are serious about your product and the relationship you are building.

I have always found this very tough to accomplish. You see, salespeople are competitive, and that can get in the way of what we are going to discuss in this chapter. While I love the passion and competition in my fellow colleagues and myself, it can also lead to the demise of our careers. We have to know when to step back, and let the non-sales team members close the deal.

The first thing we must recognize is that we are neither the smartest nor the most technical people regarding our product(s). We may be pretty damn good at selling the features, however, the people or engineering teams that designed what we are selling are much smarter than us! Once we have that dialed in and understood, we can leverage their knowledge to close deals. Yes, I said it. CLOSE DEALS!! LET'S GO!

I love selling; I love trying to be technical. But I know that I am not nearly as technical as some of my counterparts. I am always trying to calculate how to bring an engineer on the call, and how to get them in the mix in the meeting. Engineers, or techs, are really good about asking blunt, hard-hitting questions that come off unassuming since they are "trying to gather information".

When we have the ability to bring a technical individual into our sales process, we need to take advantage of this. I know some salespeople absolutely cringe at this. What if they say something they shouldn't or aren't perfect with their words? That is totally fine, and in fact can be beneficial. ***It humanizes our sales process*** and our company. It adds value to our organization and validates our company in our respective industry and space.

The medical industry has used this tactic for years by hiring medical specialists such as nurses, pharmacists or physicians; they are most often referred to as medical liaisons. The model is fairly simple; arrange a big meeting with an important prospect or customer and bring these knowledge wealthy colleagues to the table to aid in closing our business. When a surgeon has a conversation with a fellow health care provider, it takes the conversation to another level. They start speaking a different language and can have more in-depth conversations. It helps build the surgeon's trust in the product since another medical professional can vouch for and evaluate the data to back up the product.

This is not only applicable to the medical industry. In fact, it can be used in ANY industry. We can bring software engineers, product engineers, technicians, etc. to the table to aid in our ability to close a deal.

Now that we understand what taking a step back means, let's evaluate how to execute the process. This is often the most difficult part. We value our account or customer as "our baby" – we grew the account and established the relationship, so we want to have control and recognition that WE grew the business. Sales people are prideful, which is essential to fuel our competitive drive. However, **_we must not forget that we are all the same team_**, and we all benefit from closing a deal!

The key to utilizing non-sales team members is recognizing when a customer has questions that are beyond the scope of the sale. As salespeople we want to have all of the answers for our customers, but we have to be careful not to speak to technology, products, or literature that we do not fully understand. After all, one of the worst things we could do is make a false claim or lie about our product(s) capabilities, whether that lie is intentional or out of ignorance. Recognizing these questions or needs from our customers allows us to effectively utilize our non-sales specialists.

Once we have established the need to bring in the experts and have identified the right technical people to bring to the table, we must facilitate proper conversation to get us from point A to point B. To optimize the meeting time for our technical team member and our customer, we need to fully brief our technician on the history and details of our customer's situation. This doesn't necessarily mean to tell our technician how to sell or close. They will do that indirectly by validating our organization. Instead, share a brief history of your business with the customer and explain the type of information the customer is asking for.

When our technician is prepared on the details of the account and what we are trying to accomplish, we make all parties aware of who will be attending the meeting. After proper introductions, we assume the norms of the sales process until we find a good place where our specialist can add value. We just don't introduce our tech and voila we get a sale! We must go through the proper sales process and continue to qualify the sale and uncover needs. Remember to peel back the onion. When the opportunity arises for us to pass the torch, we do so in a confident way. If a customer asks a technical related question to me, I usually lead in with "Mike, what are your thoughts? You have had really good experience with project "x" and this seems very similar."

I worked with an outside sales rep that was absolutely incredible at this. He was not technical at all; in fact, he was below where we liked most of the reps to be. However, he was the best at stepping back. He brought more deals to our company than any other outside sales rep. He also knew when and how to bring technical team members to the meeting. This skill helped him triple his sales territory in three years!

Understand when the right time to bring a technical person into the sales cycle is. Don't be the person that always feels the need to bring someone in to every meeting. Alternatively, don't be the person that is too prideful and knows everything. Technical people are great selling tools. They allow the sales person to take a step back and let their counterparts validate their company or product. ***Step back like a savage!***

Key Action Items for "When to Step Back"

1. Identify the specialists in your organization and their respective roles
2. Find a couple key prospects or accounts that you can utilize a technician in
3. Schedule a meeting with a technical individual, but with a solidified customer
4. Properly utilize a technician in prospect
5. Close a deal with a tech by your side!

The Value of No

"No!"

No is such a powerful word in nearly every language! It is also a word that should be intertwined in every successful sales professional's vocabulary. Unfortunately, we do not use this word enough. But the truth is, no is extremely important to the sales process, the sales cycle and the overall health and strategic planning of a company's success.

Saying no can have many positive implications. Let's walk through a few important lessons and examples that will allow us to add more value to our customers and our organization through the use of the word "no".

It is actually possible to be too accommodating with our customers. As sales professionals, our customers push us every day, and that is a good thing! When our customers push us for a better lead-time, a lower price, better service etc., it challenges us to be better – and there is nothing wrong with that! However, **_we do not have to say YES to everything_** they ask for. We must remember every time we comply with a customer request or need, we are setting a precedent, and it can be dangerous if we aren't paying attention.

I learned this the hard way. I was blindsided by the CEO of mid-size business during a meeting. She had some wild claims about my company she had learned from a competitor of mine– nothing new in the selling world. A couple of weeks later she requested that we send her a weekly report of what products her customers were receiving from us. Desperate to save and keep the account, I complied with her request. I bent over backwards to make sure she got that report every week, including while I was on vacation. Every time I sent the report, a red flag raised in my head; was it really that hard for them to obtain and track their own data? It turned out it was difficult for them to track this, and they were utilizing my report for decisions for their own self-interest. Six months later, I received a phone call from a manager at the organization informing me they were working with a different company and going to try to start their own "business". Fair enough, I lost – it happens in the sales world. Walk down the road a few months later, and we start learning they are moving the customers that I provided on the weekly report to their newly created company. I just jump started their start up business with a base they could leverage!

Looking back, it is easy to see I was going to lose the business either way. However, I was so desperate and accommodating that I made the situation much worse. If I had said "no" (in a professional manner) it would have decreased the impact to my organization. Don't get me wrong; it would have been extremely difficult to say no. I felt intimidated and somewhat coerced into complying with their demands. Instead of letting them force me into doing something that made me uncomfortable, I needed to accept the fact that at that point the business was gone; I needed to cut my ties and go home to fight another day. This was a tough lesson to learn, but I am so pumped up that I learned it early in my career and will avoid that mistake in the future.

We need to be able to make the tough decisions, and sometimes that starts and ends with no. We all have the customer that asks us to participate in a project that may be out of our company's scope of business. Often these projects are extremely difficult to complete and require endless amounts of company time and resources. Being in sales, we tend to accept the challenge thinking we can conquer this obstacle; we are competitive! While it is extremely important to push our company to remain innovative for our customers, we are walking a fine line when we entertain these deals. It is important to hear our customers' requests, but we need to be able to cut the cord quickly if it is not in our company's best interest!

An easy and quick way to weed these projects out is to require an NRE fee, or a non-recurring engineering fee. If our customer doesn't blink and agrees or entertains the idea of an NRE, we can take that as a great sign that we can continue to the next step of the project. If they decide not to entertain the idea of an NRE, that may be a sign they are not as invested in the project as we originally thought, and we may need to cut ties with the project.

If we are not in a position to propose an NRE fee, we need to do an extremely good job of uncovering needs and identifying how those needs fit within our organization and as a part of our business plan. We are the first line of defense related to qualifying and vetting opportunities as they come to us. If we aren't completely certain about a deal or customer request, we need to err on the side of caution and bring in other team members for their input. And ultimately, if we determine this is not a good fit or decision for our company, we need to be able to pull the plug. It can be challenging to decline a customer's request while remaining professional and keeping the opportunity for future business open. An example of how to say no in this situation could be to say, "Unfortunately I am going to have to say no as this is not a great fit for our organization at this time. However, if you have a similar project or additional questions in the future, please reach back out – I will provide a quick and timely response." Our customers value their time as well, and they appreciate it much more if we can say no quickly rather than drag a project on just to turn it down in the end.

Don't we love it when customers walk all over us?! It happens all the time, and sometimes it is warranted, no question. However, when we have the constant abuse by the same customer, we need to evaluate our relationship and set some parameters. A perfect example of this is the lack of communication from a customer on our expectations to perform. There are times when we execute our communication really well with a certain customer, however, they don't take accountability for their lack of communication and want us to make it up on our end. They may want us to discount our product or pay for shipping. These are fair claims if we happen to goof up. However, if this is a one-sided relationship and our customer refuses to take accountability but requires us to always "make it right" we need to evaluate that customer. I am not necessarily talking about just the one time this happens with a customer. I am talking about the habitual offender that constantly nags at us and refuses to take accountability. We must set a precedent with them so we do not continue to see recurring issues. **_We cannot be afraid of our customers;_** instead, we need to have a professional conversation. If we do not have these conversations, the relationship and customer will become extremely artificial and easier to lose. **_Learn how to say no like a savage!_**

Key Action Items for "The Value of No"

1. Fully grasp and understand you are able to say "no" to your customer
2. Decide if you can utilize an NRE strategy

3. Become a quick decision maker evaluating if a project is feasible
4. Set a professional precedent with your customers
5. Don't be afraid of your customers – be a value-add resource

Passion

"You better learn to like it."

My college golf coach shared these words of wisdom with me as I complained about how terrible I was at putting and how much I hated it. I understood what he was saying; if I didn't get better at putting, I wasn't going to improve my game. So I tricked myself into liking it. I ate, slept, and breathed putting. And in a real psychopath move, I tucked my putter into bed at night with me on a few occasions. Was I the best putter on the team after that? Not even close, but I did improve enough to start traveling with the team and playing in tournaments. Finding, or forcing, a passion for putting elevated my overall performance on the course.

Passion is so essential to selling successfully. It is extremely difficult to be a top salesperson for your organization if you do not have a passion for what you are doing or what you are selling. And, as my shared experience shows you, **_there is such a thing as "learned passion"_** – if you don't have the enthusiasm you think you should today, it doesn't mean you can't develop that in the future. Putting became a learned passion for me, and it elevated my game enough to start performing at a high level. So, if you don't have a passion for what you are selling today, focus on finding and developing your passion for your industry or your selling strategy. Your other option is to dust off your resume and find a new company to work for – and that is okay, not every job is for everyone.

There are two major areas you need to find passion for. The first is your company, culture, product etc. It is extremely important to find a passion in what we are selling as an organization and to believe in the culture and the company direction. We need to be passionate about our company roadmap, our sales process and who we are in our respective industry. If we cannot find a passion for our product or company's mission, we need to work on developing a learned passion. Try talking with other people you work with to gain insight into the product's benefits or the drive behind the company's mission. This is important, because if we can't buy into what we are selling, how will our customer? Once we develop a learned passion, our customers can feel that energy, and we can see an increase in our sales results! Have excitement for what you do. Be energetic, be honest, and have more passion than your competitor!

Another important area to find passion in sales is in the many qualities that make sales professionals successful. It is possible to love a lot of these areas of selling, but dislike one or two of them. I imagine that some of you love building relationships, you are great at follow-up, or you love traveling to have meetings with your customers. However, you may not enjoy asking tough questions. Maybe you don't like asking which vendor a prospect/lead is currently using. This is an extremely common theme in the sales process as it is uncomfortable.

I never enjoyed asking the tough questions. There were times when customers would lie to my face saying they used my company, when of course they had not, and I didn't ever challenge them on this! My manager was with me on one of these occasions, and he did not appreciate how I passively handled the situation. He taught me when we challenge a customer it doesn't need to be rude or unprofessional. We can handle this professionally and even have a little fun while doing it. I learned how to manage these situations by simply flashing a smile and stating "Our company? Are you sure about that? You wouldn't be mixing me up with Joe (competitor) would you? He's a better-looking guy than me, so I can't imagine you would do that." We all have similar scenarios that come up rather often. Find an effective way to communicate or challenge your customer that doesn't come off awkwardly.

Asking these tough questions was a learned passion for me and is something I continue to improve upon. However, developing a learned passion in this area has allowed me to have more difficult conversations with my customer and handle them professionally. Digging into tough aspects gives us more information about our customers, and it allows us to add more value to them as we can understand their needs better.

Realize that it is totally normal to not have a passion in every aspect of the sales process. We need to understand and identify our weaknesses and develop a detailed plan to develop a learned passion in order to become a more effective and efficient sales professional. Remember, customers can tell when we aren't fully invested in the process. ***Have the passion of a savage!***

Key Action items for "Passion"

1. Identify what we are passionate about within the sales process
2. Realize if we have passion for our current organization
3. Understand if we need to develop learned passions for our organization
4. Develop a plan for learned passion in our sales weaknesses
5. Have more passion than all of our competitors

Burying the Competition

"When you are winning, don't go easy on them. Step on their throats."

This may sound ruthless to some of you, but it is an important lesson in business competition. This was something my basketball coach routinely told us during games. He challenged us to put forward maximum effort until the final horn sounded. As sales professionals, I would wager to bet most of you love to compete and you love to win.

Winning in sales is much like winning in every other competition. To be successful, we have to do a multitude of things that lead us to become successful and ultimately take market share away from our competitors. ***When we start taking market share from competition, we***

need to leverage that momentum and snowball our efforts to maximize our success. I am going to put a little different spin on how we effectively bury our competition.

There is an old saying; keep your friends close, and your enemies closer. Every sales professional should take this and stuff it in their back pocket. How can you use this to your advantage? There are a number of things I do or have done to understand how my competition thinks. I am going to share a few of the items that helped me become more successful against my competition.

I check my competition out on Facebook. My college roommates would classify this as "Facebook creeping". Whatever it is called, it can be used to help you understand your competition. You can gather a ton of information on social media. For example, let's say one of your competitors went to the University of Nebraska, and one of your clients is a huge Husker football fan. That could be a cause for concern on the relationship side. But if we are aware of this, we can work to find strategies to minimize that advantage of our competitor. Taking it one step further, we can check out our competitor's "friends" and see if any of our customers are friends with our competitor – this may be a sign they are cheating on us. This can be used on multiple different types of social media sites. It provides a ton of information that can help us understand our competition. If you pay close enough attention, you can catch them posting photos on a vacation and swoop in and steal their business. I have actually done this before, and it legitimately worked. Trust me, social media can be a huge key to selling success!

Do you want to see how successful one of your competitors is? A simple, but not foolproof way to do this is to look them up on the county assessment page and see what kind of house they live in. This will allow you a chance to see what kind of lifestyle they are living. Keep in mind, there are many factors that can contribute to their house size, but it does allow you to evaluate what their success may be in your current geographic area.

Have you ever heard of Crunchbase or Manta? Manta provides a range of revenue and industry estimate for private companies. They also provide information on where the company is located and key executives. Crunchbase is an online platform where you can type in your competitor's company name and see financial information about them. It shows you how much funding they have received, when they raised funding, who the CEO is, where their location is, who is on their Board of Directors, links to SEC forms, and what industry they are in. I dove down a rabbit hole on a competitor a few months ago on Crunchbase. I learned that the competition I was researching recently filed an SEC form trying to raise $275,000. My first question was, why wouldn't they leverage that debt with a bank to save equity? I also saw they had only raised $200,000 and their minimum investment requirement was $10,000. In a fifteen-year-old company, these were major red flags; it appeared they were not doing well financially.

How about Similarweb? Similarweb is an absolutely incredible tool, and it's free! Similarweb gives you access to see how many page views a website receives per month. It also provides data trends, as well as referring and referral websites. It gives industry ranks, which can be somewhat difficult to decipher but can be useful. This is powerful knowledge to evaluate how effective our competition really is.

If you are in medical sales, or any sales that allows you to be in the same place quite often (every week or two), the next item we are going to discuss is applicable to you. If you pull into an account's parking lot, and you don't want any surprises while you are in there, start learning what your competition drives! I know what car nearly all my competitors drive. If I happen to run into them while at an account, I physically write down the time and day of the week they are there. I want to understand their routine, if they have one. Sometimes when I see their car in a parking lot, I may high tail it to one of their other accounts since I know they aren't there and try to take some business.

Have you ever called one of your accounts on the phone and blocked your phone number? I have done this and actually heard a number of colleagues that have utilized this. It is a simple task. Call your customer from a restricted number and ask them what they use for "enter your product here". Sometimes they may say, I use company "x" and it happens to be your company! Or we could come to find out it is our competition. This is an easy, effective tool that should be utilized often.

All of the above are just a few tools that help us understand and crush our competitors. We can better understand who our competitors are and their character via their social media. We can utilize public information available through certain websites to understand the financial health of our competitors' companies. We also have the ability to see how successful our individual competitors are. This information is immensely helpful when used appropriately. We can effectively bury our competition if we know how they think and act, believe me! ***<u>Bury the competition like a savage!</u>***

Key Action Items for "Bury the Competition"

1. Understand who your top competitors are
2. Research them on various social media sites
3. Plug your competitor's company information in the websites mentioned
4. Gather all of this information to better understand your competitor's behavior
5. Make business decisions based on the learned information

Coffee is for CLOSERS

"Coffee is for CLOSERS."

I say this to my team quite often – and I guarantee you they think I am cheesy for it. But I absolutely love it! In this section, we are going to discuss advancing the sale and closing deals. There are so many misperceptions about closing that we need to understand.

We have all watched some sort of movie where the main character can close like an absolute savage. But I am sure I don't have to remind you, movies are often not true! Closing a sale is not this hot, tense moment of sweat and boiler room action. It is not forceful, rude or threatening. Closing is somewhat of an art, and quite frankly, it can be very simple!

I want to be clear about something. Sometimes we don't have the opportunity to close the sale in a meeting. The executive board may not have approved funding yet, or our customer's product may not be approved. We need to ask key questions so we can understand if it is viable for us to close the business. If it isn't, that is perfectly fine; let's focus on advancing the sale. We need to have considerable self-awareness here. I have seen people lose a deal because they ask for a PO, yet our customer is not in a given state to issue one. **_Advancing the sale is the next best thing to closing_** – let's keep the deal alive.

Closing a sale must always consist of asking for the business. If we do not ask for the business, we aren't showing interest or commitment to our prospect. Asking for the business can be as easy as, "What do I need to do to earn your business?" This is a highly effective component to inform our prospect that we are interested in earning their business.

If a prospect is currently using a competitor, we can ask them to give us a shot one time. "Just give me one shot. If we stink and you don't like us, you can always go back to the incumbent." I have used this line quite a few times; I would bet it worked in over half of the accounts I used it in.

When it is used genuinely, and we have credibility with our prospect, you will be surprised how often this is successful.

Outside of asking for the business or asking what we need to do to earn the business, we need to have a number of key qualities that allow us to close a deal. Most of the deals we close have a long sales cycle. In a long sales cycle, we must have effective and timely communication with our prospect. We need to follow up multiple times and make sure we set reminders in our calendar. Making visits to our customer is an effective tool that has proven successful as well. Again, this shows our customer that we are serious in closing the deal and earning their business.

Let's not make closing more difficult than it really is! Closing is simply asking for the business. There are many ways to ask for the business, so I encourage you to get comfortable with a certain closing line that is easy to remember and easy to repeat. Once we close the business, it is always wise to send a hand-written thank you note, thanking our customer for allowing us the opportunity to be their vendor. Hopefully it is a customer with multiple projects, as this will bode well with our NEW customer! Get out there and ***close deals like a savage!***

Key Action Items for Coffee is For Closers

1. Are you close to closing, or advancing the sale? Have self-awareness
2. Don't be afraid to advance the sale if you can't close
3. Ask what you can do to earn the business
4. Ask an account that is using your competitor to give you a shot
5. Once you close the deal – send a note to your customer

To the reader: I understand your time is valuable. I appreciate you taking time to read this book. I hope you learned at least one tip on how to effectively grow your sales career. Thank you for allowing me the opportunity to share my stories with you. ← See what I did there?!. Tell a friend about this book!

Made in the USA
Middletown, DE
16 October 2018